CALLING ALL
Deborahs
ALL

WORKBOOK

LINDA P. JONES

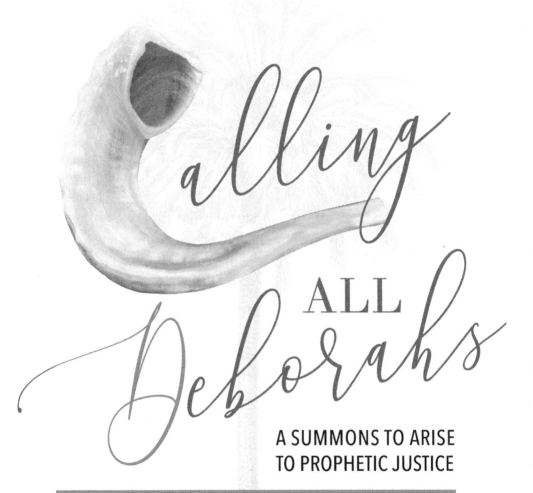

alling

ALL

Deborahs

**A SUMMONS TO ARISE
TO PROPHETIC JUSTICE**

WORKBOOK

GLORIOUS WORKS
PUBLISHING

Calling All Deborahs Workbook
by Linda P. Jones

Unless otherwise noted, all Scripture quotations from the Holy Bible, and are taken from the New King James Version and King James Versions of the Holy Bible © 1979, 1980, 1982 by Thomas Nelson Inc.

Published by Glorious Works Publishing
Cover Design by Kainos Creative Studios
Book Design and Layout by Kainos Creative Studios
Editing by Paula Richards of Eagle's Eye Editing Services

ISBN 978-976-96300-1-7

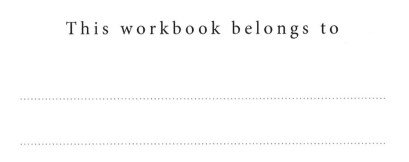

This workbook belongs to

....

....

I am a modern-day Deborah!

Contents

Introduction xi

Sᴇssɪᴏɴs

1   Deborahs of the Past 1

2   The Phases of the Times of the Judges 7

3   The Prevailing Conditions at the Time of Deborah . . . 17

4   The Private Life of Deborah 23

5   The Public Life of Deborah 31

6   The Performance of Deborah's Ministry   41

7   The War Plan of Deborah Part 1 49

8   The War Plan of Deborah Part 2 55

9   The Pampering Mother   63

10 The Provoking of the Jael Anointing 69

Epilogue: In Praise of Modern-Day Deborahs 75

About the Author 79

Introduction

The purpose of this workbook is to encourage you to put the lessons learnt in Calling All Deborahs into practice. It was written to energize and empower the call of God on your life and to incite a movement of Deborahs to action to see that God's righteousness and justice are brought to bear in every sphere of society.

This workbook is great for individuals, or workshops, small groups, bible study groups whether at home gatherings or in official church ministries. It will help individuals to redefine how they see themselves and the call to prophetic justice, and they will take a quantum leap forward to impact and influence society wherever they are called to be salt and light. It may be in the family, or fashion industry, the Ecclesia, government, education, science, business, media, arts & entertainment, etc.

I invite you to honestly engage the questions and activations in this workbook with intentionality and allow the Holy Spirit to speak to you. For the best result read each corresponding chapter before you answer the related questions. The Holy Spirit will open your ear to hear and empower you to implement His strategic counsel for your sphere of influence so that ultimately, the kingdoms of this world will become the kingdoms of our Lord, and of His Christ; and He shall reign forever and ever.

Awake, awake, Deborahs! *"Your King is calling you out from the shadows and calling you into His marvelous light to establish justice and redemption to the generations"* (Christy Johnston).

— Linda P. Jones

session 1

Deborahs of the Past

"Because I delivered the poor who cried out, the fatherless and the one who had no helper. The blessing of a perishing man came upon me, and I caused the widow's heart to sing for joy. I put on righteousness, and it clothed me; my justice was like a robe and a turban. I was eyes to the blind, and I was feet to the lame. I was a father to the poor, and I searched out the case that I did not know. I broke the fangs of the wicked, and plucked the victim from his teeth."

Job 29:12-17

The *Call of Deborah* is not necessarily a new one, many women in the past have heard and responded to the call to see that justice and righteousness be granted to the poor, the underprivileged, the broken, the widows, the orphans, the homeless, the oppressed... Many have stood against the moral decay, depravity, lawlessness, prejudice, and injustices in the nations of the earth; and they did so at great cost to them and even their families. Some have even lost their lives for the cause of justice and rightness, but their contributions have not gone unnoticed. Through their voices, protests, and their selfless contributions and sacrifices, they have caused: legislation to be changed, hospitals and learning institutions to be built for the advancement and support large numbers of members of society, who otherwise would not have had that privilege. By and large these 'Deborahs' have literally transformed society.

It is a privilege to join the ranks of those who hear and answer the call of the Deborahs.

Some paid the ultimate price with their lives, but they counted the cost, put their hand to the plow and did not look back. If we listen closely we could almost hear them cheering us on to follow in their footsteps to answer the call of the Deborahs.

CALLED OUT QUOTE
Calling All Deborahs Chapter 1

FOR REFLECTION & DISCUSSION

1 Do you hear the call of the Deborahs? What steps are you actively taking to fulfill that call?

....

....

....

....

....

....

2 Search out some accounts of other Deborahs of the past and discuss how their obedience has impacted society even to today.

....

....

....

....

....

....

....

....

3 Name and discuss other biblical Deborahs who answered the call and the outcome of their obedience.

....

....

....

....

....

....

....

4 The call of Deborah is a call that requires a lifestyle of righteousness; therefore, we must ensure that we are not in any way walking in compromise. If you need to, take time to examine your heart and then pray saying this simple prayer.

Heavenly Father, I submit my life to You. Let the searchlight of Your Spirit expose every area of my heart that needs to be cleansed from any unrighteousness. Fill my heart with Your love for holiness and justice and most of all Your love. In Jesus' Mighty Name, Amen.

Add your own words if you wish:

....

....

....

....

....

....

....

session 2

The Phases of the Times of the Judges

The Book of Judges is the account of Israel after the death of Joshua and the elders who followed the Lord (Judges 1:1). More so, it is an account of the establishing of God's righteous justice in the land, first, against the sin of disobedience and idolatry of His people, and secondly, to bring down the wicked and oppressive rule of the principalities set against God's people.

Unfortunately, it is a book of defeat and disgrace, *"as every man did that which was right in his own eyes"*. Instead of driving out the pockets of resistance from enemy heathen nations within their boundaries, subduing them and fully possessing their inheritances as the Lord commanded, the children of Israel mixed with the heathen nations and adopted their idolatrous practices. This greatly angered the Lord and it became necessary for Him to chasten His people. They were plagued from the enemies within their boundaries and enemy nations surrounding them. Their lives became one vicious cycle – from rest to sin, to rebellion, reckoning, repentance, renewal and rest again (See Chart below).

Under the rule of the judges, the children of Israel would experience a time of prolonged rest. For example, when the Lord raised up Othniel, who delivered them from the oppression of King of Mesopotamia, the land had rest for 40 years. However, as soon as that judge died, the children of Israel rebelled against the Lord, they returned to their evil ways of spiritual whoredom – and the cycle would continue all over again (Judges 2:10-23) describes in more detail the pattern of the cycle of the children of Israel.

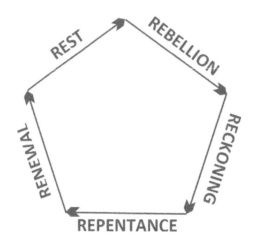

The different phases of the times of the Judges

- REST

"And Israel served the Lord all the days of Joshua, and all the days of the elders who out lived Joshua, who had known all the works of the Lord which He had done for Israel." – Joshua 24:31

- REBELLION

"The children did evil in the sight of the Lord and served the Baals and they forsook the Lord God of their fathers...they followed other gods from among the gods of the people who were all around them, and they bowed down to them and provoked the Lord to anger." – Judges 2:11-12 (Generational)

- RECKONING

"And the anger of the Lord was hot against Israel. So He delivered them into the hands of plunderers who despoiled them and He sold them into the hands of their enemies all around, so that they could no longer stand before their enemies." – Judges 2:14

- REPENTANCE

"And the children of Israel cried out to the lord, saying, 'We have sinned against You, because we have both forsaken our God and served the Baals!" – Judges 10:10

- RENEWAL

"And when the Lord raised up judges for them, the Lord was with the judge and delivered them out of the hand of their enemies all the days of the judge; for the Lord was moved to pity by their groaning because of those who oppressed them and harassed them." – Judges 2:18

- REST

And the land had rest for..."

FOR REFLECTION & DISCUSSION

1 Review the chart of the cycle of rebellion in Israel. Was there a time in your life when you disobeyed God and was out of alignment with His will? Describe how your heart was turned around to restoration and to rest.

....

....

....

....

....

....

2 The Lord was furiously angry at the children of Israel and thus He withdrew His protection and power from them and delivered them into the hands of their foreign oppressors.

   a. What are your personal thoughts on God's anger towards His people?

....

....

....

....

....

....

....

....

b. What does the Scripture have to say about God's anger towards His people?

....

....

....

....

....

....

....

....

3 One of the reasons the anger of the Lord was hot against Israel is because they defiled the land by embracing sinful idolatrous practices. Can you identify some modern-day sinful idolatrous practices the Church has embraced?

....

....

....

....

....

....

4 Describe the political, moral, and spiritual climate of your community, city, state, or nation that is a source of concern to you.

....

....

....

....

....

....

....

5 Identify some injustices that deeply affect you, whether in your family, at work, the educational system, in a ministry you are presently in, or the government?

....

....

....

....

....

....

6 What are some steps you would take in addressing the situation(s) you identified above?

....

....

....

....

....

....

....

7 How far are you willing to go with those steps if and when opposition arises?

....

....

....

....

....

....

....

This was the sorry state
of the people of God in
Israel, and though we
criticise them for their
behavior, it is sad to say
that in many ways the
church of Jesus Christ,
His Body, His Bride,
oftentimes behaves in
much the same manner.

CALLED OUT QUOTE
Calling All Deborahs Chapter 2

session 3

The Prevailing Conditions at the Time of Deborah

"When Ehud was dead, the children of Israel again did evil in the sight of the LORD. So the LORD sold them into the hand of Jabin king of Canaan, who reigned in Hazor. The commander of his army was Sisera, who dwelt in Harosheth Hagoyim. And the children of Israel cried out to the LORD; for Jabin had nine hundred chariots of iron, and for twenty years he had harshly oppressed the children of Israel...Village life ceased, it ceased in Israel, until I, Deborah arose, arose a mother in Israel"

Judges 4:1-3; 5:7

I t wasn't long after the last judge passed that Israel went back to their rebellious ways, *doing evil in the sight of the Lord*, and so God handed them into the hand of Jabin king of Canaan, who, with the commander of the army, Sisera, mercilessly and cruelly oppressed them. The Canaanite was given legal right to take hold of the people and bring them into humiliating subjugation.

FOR REFLECTION & DISCUSSION

1 *"God sold them into the hand of..."* This was His response to the people's outright rebellion and hardheartedness; He allowed them to fall into the hands of their enemies. These enemies in reality were governed by oppressive demonic forces. What are your thoughts of a loving God acting this way?

....

....

....

....

....

....

....

2 Is there a New Testament example where something similar occurred? Read the entire chapter and then discuss what that meant.

....

....

....

....

....

....

....

....

....

3 Below is a list of the effects that the Canaanite spirit can have on individuals and even a nation, as we saw in the case of the children of Israel. Circle the one you can identify with.

    a.   Intimidation and Fear

    b.   Economic

    c.   Social

    d.   Spiritual

4 From the description and operation of the Canaanite spirit, can you identify these effects in your family, in your own leadership style of dealing with others, and in your nation? If yes, state what steps you can take to overcome these deficiencies.

....

....

19

....

....

....

....

....

5 What measures would you take to guard your heart against its influence?

....

....

....

....

....

....

....

....

The children of Israel were in a land given to them to possess. Rather than dispossess their enemies, they were being oppressed by them. It is a bitter lesson to learn that when you don't destroy what God says to destroy in your life it will live to become thorns in your flesh or worse yet, destroy you.

CALLED OUT QUOTE
Calling All Deborahs Chapter 3

session 4

The Private Life of Deborah

T though very little is said about Deborah's life behind the scenes, we can conclude that everyday village life situations were obviously her classroom. She was being tutored by the Holy Spirit through life's tough lessons for her public office; perhaps hostility and various circumstances were used to test her attitude, self-control, her tenacity, resolve, while remaining compassionate toward others. Deborah's identity was formed, and her assignment clarified in the secret place. Every Deborah must have a private life where she will be formed, framed, and trained to be presented on the world stage.

FOR REFLECTION & DISCUSSION

1 Describe one life-changing experience you have had in your secret
place. How has it impacted your life?

....

....

....

....

....

....

....

2 Meditate on the following Scriptures speaking of God as our Rock,
and record how these scriptures impacted you and what the Holy
Spirit highlighted to you.

- Deuteronomy 32:4

....

....

....

....

....

....

....

- Psalm 18:2

....

....

....

....

....

....

- Psalm 27:5

....

....

....

....

....

....

....

- Psalm 32:7

....

....

....

....

....

....

- Psalm 91:1-4

....

....

....

....

....

....

....

- 1 Corinthians 10:4

....

....

....

....

....

....

3 Discuss the bee-like qualities of Deborah and how they equipped her for her assignment.

....

....

....

....

....

....

....

4 It is impossible to have intimacy without obedience. What do you understand by this?

....

....

....

....

....

....

....

5 Deborah waited in the presence of God. How are you preparing yourself in this waiting period?

....

....

....

....

....

....

6 "Identity must precede assignment". What does this mean to you? Do you have clarity on your true identity in Christ?

....

....

....

....

....

....

7 Search the Scriptures for verses that speak about your identity in Christ, meditate on them. List a few below.

• ....

• ....

• ....

• ....

• ....

Deborah, the bee, made her home in God her Rock; He was her hiding place. A Deborah has to have a place where it is just her and God alone; you can't bring anybody in there with you.

CALLED OUT QUOTE
Calling All Deborahs Chapter 4

30

session 5

The Public Life of Deborah

> "NOW Deborah, a prophetess, the wife of Lapidoth, was judging Israel at that time."
>
> Judges 4:4

Certain segments of the religious world have felt that the best way to serve God is living a monastic life – 'come out from among them and be separate' they say. But the Lord has called us to live a life that is relational and impactful; we are called to be the salt and the light of the earth. Salt must mix with food in order to give it flavor and light must be shone in darkness to appreciate its full effect. Deborah had a hidden life, but she lived a very public life as well – she was a woman who took personal and active interest in the needs of the people of her community. She lived out in public what she received in private. She was a woman on an assignment – she was called by God to be prophetess, and judge at a critical time in the life of the nation of Israel, while remaining faithful in her call as wife of Lapidoth.

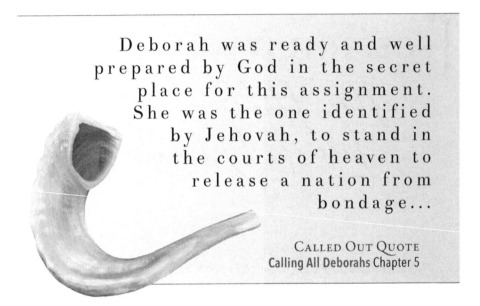

Deborah was ready and well prepared by God in the secret place for this assignment. She was the one identified by Jehovah, to stand in the courts of heaven to release a nation from bondage...

CALLED OUT QUOTE
Calling All Deborahs Chapter 5

FOR REFLECTION & DISCUSSION

Deborah The Prophetess

Deborah was a down-to-earth community woman who connected with the people and her neighbourhood. She exercised her prophetic gift, borne out of her times of intimacy with the Lord, to minister to the needs of the people.

1 What is your understanding of the prophetic gifting and prophesying?

....

....

....

....

....

....

2 Are you practicing the prophetic gifting by prophesying to people? Who have you prophesied to recently, and how did the person respond?

....

....

....

....

....

....

....

3 Do you have to function in the office of a prophet to prophesy? Verify your answer with scriptural evidence.

....

....

....

....

....

....

4 What is it that you are doing right now that would qualify you for being called to prophesy?

....

....

....

....

....

....

....

Deborah, the Wife of Lapidoth

1 The call of God supersedes one's gender, nationality, age, marital or socio-economic status. The call of God has to do with whom He chooses. Do you agree? Substantiate your answer with scriptures.

....

....

....

....

....

....

....

2 How do you feel about a woman being called to public ministry and not her husband?

....

....

....

....

....

....

....

3 What precedent do you find in scripture where a woman was called to leadership role and not the man?

....

....

....

....

....

....

....

4 Those who cannot come under authority should not exercise authority over others. Do you agree? State the reasons for your answer.

....

....

....

....

....

....

Deborah, the Judge

1 What do you understand by the phrase 'righteous judgment'?

....

....

....

....

....

....

....

2 God trusted Deborah to administer judgment and justice to His people with a heart of compassion. Could He trust you to make just/ righteous decisions in alignment with His heart?

....

....

....

3 What characteristics is He looking for in such a person?

....

....

....

....

....

....

....

4 Are those characteristics of leadership growing in you? Discuss how.

....

....

....

....

....

....

5 How can you develop more of those characteristics?

....

....

....

session 6

The Performance of Deborah's Ministry

"She would sit under the palm tree of Deborah between Ramah and Bethel in the mountains of Ephraim. And the children of Israel came up to her for judgment."

Judges 4:5

It is important to reiterate that it is only out of the hidden place – time spent in intimacy with the Lord, that Deborah could have successfully functioned in ministry. How she performed ministry was the fruit of the hidden life. The right position is everything.

FOR REFLECTION & DISCUSSION

1 Deborah operated from a position of rest. How do you respond when all around you is in turmoil? Do you find it difficult to abide in the rest of God?

....

....

....

....

....

....

....

2 Search the Scriptures and discover at least five verses that speak about the rest and/or the peace God has provided for us in the midst of chaos.

• ....

• ....

• ....

- ....
- ....

3 Deborahs of today cannot be distracted or dissuaded by societal prejudices or cultural norms; they have to know what or where is their 'palm tree' – their place of function. Are you able to identify what is your 'palm tree'? Describe your palm tree.

....

....

....

....

....

....

....

....

....

....

4 Spend some time studying the many characteristics and significance of the palm tree and make note of some of the deep truths it holds for you.

....

....

....

....

....

5 Deborah was reliable; every day she could be found under the palm tree. Can you be found at the same 'place'; not moody but consistent and trustworthy, living a life of integrity?

....

....

....

....

....

6 In the midst of a society of decay and brokenness, where do we live? How does the symbolism of Ramah, Bethel and Ephraim character-ize your life? Discuss the impact of the symbolism of each place and how they relate to your life now and your relationship with the Lord.

- Ramah

....

....

....

....

- Bethel

....

....

....

....

- Ephraim

....

....

....

....

7 Search out more scriptures where other individuals had significant
encounters with God on the mountains or hills.

• ....

• ....

• ....

• ....

• ....

8 We don't literally go to mountains or hills to pray or meet God as
a way of life. Then discuss how that transpires in your day to day
experience.

....

....

....

....

....

....

....

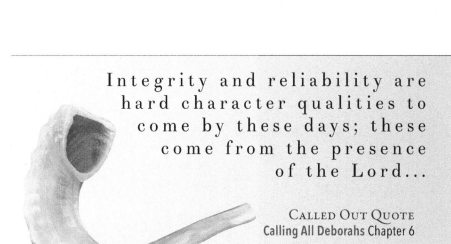

Integrity and reliability are
hard character qualities to
come by these days; these
come from the presence
of the Lord...

CALLED OUT QUOTE
Calling All Deborahs Chapter 6

session 7
The War-Plan of Deborah *Part 1*

"And she sent and called Barak son of Abinoam from Kedesh in Naphtali and said to him, has not the Lord, the God of Israel, commanded [you]"

Judges 4:6a AMP

All along Deborah was helping the people of God with their personal and spiritual lives, but the time came when her focus changed from the people to Barak. Deborah must have heard directly from God that the time had come for more decisive action against the enemies of God and His people. She saw that the task at hand was an enormous one, and she trusted completely the proven, ultimate Heavenly Team, and with their prophetic strategic counsel, she summoned Commander Barak. Ironically, Barak also means lightning – he came swiftly and without delay (Judges 5:6-9). There was no division between them as they worked together in true honor and respect, alongside each other for the purpose of God's people and the Glory of God. There was no competing, but only completing!

FOR REFLECTION & DISCUSSION

1 Timing is everything. The Lord leads us in many different ways; sometimes He gives a blueprint to follow, other times He expects us to move out by faith on the bit of revelation He has given. Describe different ways you have experienced the leading of the Lord in your life and ministry.

....

....

....

....

....

....

....

2 Recall a time that you acted outside the timing of God and what happened as a result.

....

....

....

....

....

....

....

3 Groundwork is necessary to be done before one fully engages in war. For Deborah it meant having Barak completely on board with what God commanded. What preparation needs to be done before you can fully launch out into doing what God has instructed you to do?

....

....

....

....

....

....

....

4 There is power and God's blessings when you come into agreement and work in unity. Moses had Joshua, Gideon had Purah, Esther had Mordecai, and Deborah had Barak. There are times God will assign someone to come alongside you in your assignment. Identify whom God has assigned to work with you in this season in this present assignment?

....

....

....

....

....

5 Are you sitting waiting for approval before you act on what God has called you to do?

....

....

....

....

....

6 Is there a 'Barak' in your life that you can encourage to move on with the assignment God has given them? If not find someone whom you could encourage and strengthen with life-giving words.

....

....

....

There are people who are waiting for instruction, who are waiting for the word of the Lord from the Deborahs; they will recognize the sound of the prophetic and will respond.

CALLED OUT QUOTE
Calling All Deborahs Chapter 7

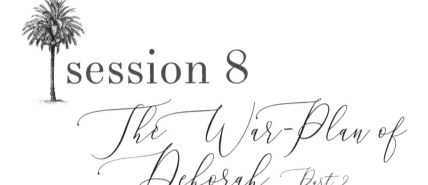

session 8

The War-Plan of Deborah Part 2

> "Go deploy troops at Mount Tabor; take with you ten thousand men of the sons of Naphtali and of the sons of Zebulun; and against you I will deploy Sisera the commander of Jabin's army, with his chariots and his multitude at the River Kishon; and I will deliver him into your hand."
>
> Judges 4:6

Deborah had tapped into the realms of heaven, between Ramah in Bethel in the mountains of Ephraim, where she received from the Lord the specific strategy for the battle. Barak was in a place of waiting. The people believed in the prophets because they knew God spoke to the prophets, 2 Chronicles 20:20 assures that if you believe in the prophet you shall prosper. There are "Baraks" who are waiting for the prophetic word from the Deborahs, and when they receive it they are going to war accordingly with it.

FOR REFLECTION & DISCUSSION

1 Deborah knew the voice of God and she did not hesitate to act. Have you ever missed the voice of God because it sounded too simple?

....

....

....

....

....

....

....

2 What are some of the ways you can increase your sensitivity to the voice of the Lord?

....

....

....

....

....

....

....

3 Living out the prophetic word spoken means you have to take action. Think back on a time you knew God gave you specific instructions to follow; document what you did and what was the outcome.

....

....

....

....

....

....

....

4 One of the recurring themes in the story of Deborah is righteousness. She lived in place of righteousness and the people were called
to deploy troops to Mt. Tabor (Judges 4:6a). Tabor, we saw signified a
place of purity.

Take some time to examine your life to ensure that it lines up with God's
standards of righteousness. This is important before you go into battle
with the enemy.

....

....

....

....

....

....

....

....

5 Because of their historical roots, rivalry could have existed between
the tribes of Naphtali and Zebulun, but God chose them to war, not
against each other, but to fight together against their common enemy. Is
there a brother or sister that you need to reconcile with so that you can
be united in love to defeat the enemy in your lives? If so, how could you
go about initiating the process?

....

....

....

....

....

....

....

6 God promises in His Word that your enemy will be His enemy, and He will fight for you. List several Scriptures that reinforce this truth, meditate and memorize them.

- ....

- ....

- ....

- ....

- ....

- ....

7 God chooses how He judges wickedness in the land. Give some examples from the Scriptures how God judged: –

a.   The wickedness of His people

....

....

....

....

....

b.   And the wickedness of the ungodly

....

....

....

....

....

We must choose our battles wisely, if not the enemy will have us distracted putting out little fires. But when we know that this is the day, then we are to act decisively.

CALLED OUT QUOTE
Calling All Deborahs Chapter 8

session 9
The Pampering Mother

After the death of Ehud and after the days of Shamgar, previous judges, for 20 years the people of God found no deliverance from their Canaanite tormentors, that is, until Deborah, a mother in Israel, arose. Scripture did not say that Deborah was a mother in the natural, but she definitely saw herself in the role of a mother to the dejected, defeated people of God. Deborah demonstrated both sides of her 'bee' personality; one of a fierce warrior against the enemies of God and the other of a caring nurturing mother to the people of God.

Today's Deborahs will be
gentle as nursing mothers
. . . but at the same time
they would be equally fierce,
audacious and aggressive
against every spirit of
wickedness that seeks to
oppress the people of God.

CALLED OUT QUOTE
Calling All Deborahs Chapter 9

FOR REFLECTION & DISCUSSION

1 How do you think Deborah knew that it was time to arise?

....

....

....

....

....

....

2 List some ways you can be a mother to someone who is hurting and depressed.

- ....

- ....

- ....

- ....

- ....

- ....

3 Deborah was not the only one who saw the state of the nation, yet she was the only one who arose to do something about it. So often we look for someone else to do something about a situation. Why do you think we do this?

....

....

....

....

....

....

....

4 What if Deborah did not arise? What if she waited for someone else to do something about the situation? What do you think would have been the outcome?

....

....

....

....

....

....

....

5 Rising up to take a stand can be costly, as in the case of Esther when she put her life on the line by deciding to appear before the King, uninvited. Esther took courage and said the famous words "If I perish, I perish." Are you ready to take a stand for injustice in your sphere of influence? And if so, where would you begin?

....

....

....

....

....

....

6 If you are going to rise up to answer the call of Deborah, there are barriers of limitations in your life that first have to be broken through. List some of the things you have to arise from in order to answer the call of Deborah.

- ....

- ....

- ....

- ....

- ....

- ....

- ....

7 I imagine that Deborah was not a woman with gaping holes in her soul; she was not walking in woundedness, thus she was able deal with the hurts and complaints of the people of God. Someone said that hurt people hurt people. Can you identify areas in your life that need healing from brokenness and pain so that you can be an effective minister? What steps can you take to receive healing?

- ....

- ....

- ....

- ....

- ....

- ....

- ....

session 10

The Provoking of the Jael Anointing

Jael the unassuming homemaker, turned mighty warrior who possessed a powerful anointing to take down the strongman. She was a king-slayer! She is a source of encouragement and empowerment to women who feel as though there is not much they can do because they are homemakers, soccer Moms and the like. Jael breathes new life and hope into women, demonstrating that God can and will partner with anyone who is prepared to partner with Him in enforcing the victory He won over Satan over 2000 years ago at Calvary's cross.

Most women become mama bears when the enemy infiltrates their family. We must remember that the enemy we are fighting today is not flesh and blood – scripture tells us that.

CALLED OUT QUOTE
Calling All Deborahs Chapter 10

FOR REFLECTION & DISCUSSION

1 It is easy to stay neutral and not get involved in other people's problems; after all, it's none of your business.

Show from Scripture instances where Jesus got involved in the other people's situations and what was the outcome.

....

....

....

....

....

....

2 Jael gave Sisera milk instead of water and when he fell asleep she took a tent pent and drove it into his temple.

How would you characterize Jael's actions? Was she justified?

....

....

....

....

....

....

....

3 Jael didn't have to ask for permission; she knew this was God. Why, do you think, this is so?

....

....

....

....

....

4 Jael had her assignment; what is yours? It is important that you keep watch so as not to miss your 'Jael moment'. Have you had any 'Jael moments' in the past? Share and discuss them.

....

....

....

....

....

....

....

5 Identify some of the present assignments God has given you to steward.

....

....

....

....

....

....

6 Are you aware of the injustices going on towards the Jewish people? List some practical ways you can help.

- ....
- ....
- ....
- ....
- ....
- ....

7 Identify what is your tent peg. You may have more than one. It may
  be praying against something happening in the school or in your
neighborhood.

- ....
- ....
- ....
- ....
- ....
- ....
- ....

Epilogue

In Praise of Modern-Day Deborahs

Most organizations or ministries were started to stand up against some form of injustice or wrongdoing that needed to be addressed. It was after a tragedy in 1980 that one mom started a movement that would significantly change the course of history in the United States. Over several years, Candace Lightner's children suffered tragic accidents from drivers impaired by drugs or alcohol. But it was after the death of her daughter Cari that Ms. Lightner promised that she would fight to make needless homicide count for something positive in years to come – she started the organization MADD – Mothers Against Drunk Drivers. With chapters across the United States of America and Canada, it is said that Candace continues to make a difference in reducing traffic crashes and saving lives. Few living people have made such a major contribution to society.

1 It will be helpful and also a source of encouragement to you to learn more about the work of other modern-day Deborahs in your com-

munity or nation, and the difference and impact they are making. Note any of particular interest to you.

....

....

....

....

....

2 Identify a current issue in your nation that is negatively affecting citizens and which you are passionate about. Assign an appropriate name for the organization that you would form to address this issue, and write its mission statement.

....

....

....

....

....

....

3 Is there any organization in your community you support? If not, maybe you can find one; do some research about its activities and how you can support it in practical ways.

....

....

....

....

....

....

....

A Charge from Heaven

"I hear a loud charge from Heaven as the daughters of righteousness are being called upon to UNITE together as an army joining in force. I see the daughters moving in powerful authority, overturning the works of darkness and injustice. There is a movement of daughters, both young and old, who are waking to the dawn of a new day. They are no longer satisfied with the status quo, no longer content to sit behind the scenes, and they are being stirred to the sound of the voice of their beloved King to move forward and take their place."

"The Holy Spirit is breathing courage, strength and purpose into them as He whispers truth to their spirits, You are here for a purpose, you have a voice and you are equipped with heavenly strategy and resolve, you are My beloved daughter and you are significant for this very hour. Do not hold back anymore."

About the Author

Rev. Linda Jones is foremost an itinerant minister who has traveled to several countries to minister the Word of God, including St. Maarten, St. Kitts, Antigua and Guyana. She is the founder of Linda P. Jones Ministries, Women of Worth Ministries, and Walking on Water Teaching & Equipping Centre. Linda is known for her gift of expository teaching of the Word of God. She also hosts a bi-monthly radio program, Words of Wisdom - 'bringing practical godly wisdom for everyday living'.

Rev. Linda P. Jones' personal mission statement is Luke 4:18-19 which is the foundational thrust for the ministries she has founded. She is passionate that individuals, especially those in the Body of Christ, are healed in every dimension (spirit soul and body) of their lives, and are adequately equipped in the Word and with the skills necessary to go and fulfill the call of God, expand the kingdom of God in the earth, and glorify Jesus Christ.

Linda holds a Bachelor of Theology from Christian International, Santa Rosa Beach Florida, and a Master of Practical Theology from Master's International University of Divinity, Evansville, Illinois, and is pursuing her doctorate in Practical Theology. Linda is a prolific writer and has authored several books which include her recent autobiography Soul Survivor, Decrees for Soul Survivor, 21-Day Devotional for Soul Survivors, The Radical Jesus...

Linda is the committed wife of Oliver and they are the parents of one daughter.

CONTACT THE AUTHOR BY

Email
lindapjones29@gmail.com *or*
womenofworthbarbados@gmail.com

Website
lindapjones.org

Facebook
http://www.facebook.com/pastorlindapjones

BOOKS BY LINDA P. JONES

Soul Survivor
21-Day Devotional for Soul Survivors
Decrees for Soul Survivor
Out of the Ashes
The Peace of God
The Radical Jesus
Exposing the Spirit of Deception
What Aileth Thee
For This Child I Prayed

Made in the USA
Columbia, SC
09 August 2021

43273455R00055